WORDS OF WISDOM

*No Fear, Plotting, Get Rid of It, Stay on The Right Course,
Relationships, Give Birth to It, Prophesy To It, and Faith*

Konsetta Kelly

Words of Wisdom

Table of Contents

Chapter 1

No Fear

When God called Jeremiah, he was afraid because he was a child. God put his word in his mouth and asked him what he saw. God showed him that he was able to do what he called him to do.

When God called Moses, he was finding excuses because he was afraid, but God already had a plan and he did exactly what God called him to do. God knows the plan for each of us and our lives, he knows the end from the beginning. He has already made a way for us. We become afraid for no reason, coming up with excuses as to why we can't do what God called us to do. We wonder how things are going to work out, but God has already taken care of it. We waste time and energy worrying about things we don't need to worry about. Slip the weight of worry off of your shoulders and let God do it in you and through you. Let Him have His way. God has already equipped us. Don't let fear hold you back or get in the way of what God wants you to do.

It's going to be your faith that carries you through. With faith, you're going to stand, with faith your business will succeed, with faith you are made whole. Whatever God wants us to do we will have to walk it with and through faith. Don't let fear hold you back from where God wants to take you. For we walk by faith and not by sight. When specific individuals got healed in the Bible, God said your faith has made you whole. Your faith works miracles. Just like the woman who had suffered from blood issues for 12 years, who pressed through the crowd to get to Jesus, saying if she could touch the hem of His garment she would be made whole. It was her faith that worked a miracle in her body to be healed. She didn't know Jesus at the time, she just heard about Him.

All you have to do is believe that it is and it's already done. Keep speaking the Word and keep believing even if it doesn't look like nothing is happening. When it looks like nothing is happening, that's when you know it is faith and when it seems like nothing is happening, God is strengthening you. Your developing patience and God is molding you and shaping you. For the next test, you'll be ready.

Who is going to stop you when you are walking in faith? The just shall live by faith. That means every day. You don't know what you're going to come up against. With faith and the authority and power that God has given you, nothing shall hurt or harm you and if God is for you, who can be against you? For greater is he that is within you than he that is in the world. You have an army of God on your side! Working on your behalf, fighting for you. Nothing shall come nigh your dwelling. It's in the name of Jesus! It's in Him we live, we move, and have our being. Deny yourself and follow after God. God wants to do something, but it's going to be your faith that's going to take you there. Don't be discouraged when you don't see it happening in your time because God's time is different from our time. God knows what he is doing and he knows what you can handle and because he has so much more for you, he has to prepare you for it. Trials come then the blessing, but in the trial, he is preparing you. We have been quarantined, shut down, stuck in the house, but God is trying to prepare us. God wants to get our attention. What have you been doing? Are you listening, are you sitting at the feet of Jesus like Mary or are you like Martha being bothered and worried about everything else? Trying to get out of the house, trying to find somewhere to go? Sit at His feet.

We have to hear from God. Blessed are those who hunger and thirst for righteousness, for they shall be filled. (Matt. 5:6) Those who seek God, those who want more of God, those who inquire of the Lord shall be filled. Seek ye first the kingdom of God and all things shall be added unto you. (Matt. 6:33) Seek to forgive, seek to love, have faith, and have joy no matter what it looks like. Seek after righteousness and be more like Christ. Seek His guidance because He will never lead you down the wrong path. We may get off course, but it's important to get back on track and follow Christ. When Jesus called Peter, Andrew, James, and John, they left everything behind and followed Christ. (Matt. 4:18-22) Sometimes we have to leave some things and people behind to follow Christ. We have to become disciples. His disciples followed Him. Where the Spirit of the Lord leads you, follow Him.

Chapter 2

Plotting - Daniel Chapter 6

Be careful when you get promoted, when your business starts to grow, or even when people compliment you. Any little thing can set the devil off. The women praised David for his 10,000 and Saul for his 1,000. This made Saul become jealous of David. Daniel was over them all and walked in an excellent Spirit. Some people around him plotted against him. There might be some people around you that are not going to like what God is doing in you and for you. Maybe family members, even your best friend can turn into your enemy, your coworkers, and so forth. You have to understand David and Saul were both good before the women praised him. In the midst of it all, keep praying, fasting, and seeking God and let him show up on your behalf. Daniel knew what was going on and how they made a decree, but he continued to pray. Don't let anybody or anything stop you from praying and worshipping God because victory is yours! They put Daniel into a lion's den thinking that it was over for him. The devil may think that he has you, but when you're walking in God, no weapon formed against you shall prosper.

God will protect you and your enemies will see what the Lord will do for you. That is why the Bible says be sober, be vigilant, because your adversary the devil roars around like a roaring lion seeking whom he may devour. (1 Peter 5:8) We have to be watchful and know what is going on and pay attention. God said he wouldn't let us be ignorant of Satan's devices. (1 Thes. 4:13-18) The king cast those men who accused Daniel into the lion's den. Not only them, but their children and their wives. Be careful if you're plotting on someone because you could be digging a hole for yourself and your family. Be careful of what you do to the children of God! Because you might be coming up against God.

Chapter 3

Get Rid of It (Mark 5:35-43)

God gave the ruler specific instructions, "Be not afraid, only believe." Jesus only took Peter, James, and John with Him. He told the people that the girl was not dead, but asleep. The people did not believe and laughed at Him, so Jesus put them out and took the father, mother, and those with Him in the room where the girl was. He took the girl by the hand and said "Arise," and the girl arose and walked. Sometimes God will give us specific instructions before he does something. He wants us to be obedient and believe. You don't need a lot of people around you, but a few believers to do what God wants to do sometimes. That is why the Bible says when two or three are gathered together in agreement, God will be there in the midst. (Matt. 18:20) The people didn't believe Jesus and laughed at Him, so God had to put them out. Some of us need to get rid of some people in our lives that don't mean so no good, who don't believe in us, and who are always negative. It becomes a time when you just have to trust, lean, and depend on God and you don't need anything messing that up.

You don't need people that are going to tear you down, but instead, you want people who build you up. We need to get rid of some of the negative thoughts we have and emotions we feel. We need to put it all out! Close the door, lock it, and never go back. Get rid of everything negative and arise in God out of our sleep and slumber. Stop taking on thoughts and battles that we don't need to take on. Sometimes we put things on ourselves and it slows us down. The Bible says to lay aside every weight and sin which would so easily beset us and run with patience the race that is set before us. (Heb. 12:1) Stop taking on things that don't matter. Arise out of your sleep! Because the only thing that matters is God and what God says about you.

Chapter 4

Stay On The Right Course (Matt. 4:8-11)

The devil will show you all the finer things in life that you think you need or want to have to get you to stray away from God. He'll show you the house, the nice cars, jewelry, shoes, purse, or anything that you would like to have if you go against God's will. The devil wants to take us off course and to do so he'll show us these things sometimes to persuade us that we'll be better if we do it his way and not God's way. Don't be fooled by the enemy because the devil knows the Word too and will try to use it against you. Don't let the devil tell you that in order for you to have these things you have to do something illegal to get it, don't let the devil tell you that you, if you are a woman, need to sleep with that man or you, if you are a man, with that woman. Don't let the devil rob you of your peace to get it. When you know what is right you do what is right. To whom much is given, much is required. (Luke 12:48)

Don't let the devil persuade you to do what is wrong. The devil will say all kinds of things to throw you off and get you to think a certain way, but the devil is a liar. Stand firm in your faith, in what you believe, and what you know in God. The enemy will try to paint a picture to make you think that it's good, but behind it is destruction. Don't be deceived by temptation. There is the lust of the flesh, lust of the eyes, and the pride of life. But God said he wouldn't have us be ignorant of Satan's devices. Be sober, be vigilant, because your adversary the devil, as a roaring lion, walketh about seeking whom he may devour. (1 Peter 5:8). Stay on the course! The race is not given to the swift nor to the strong, but to those who endure to the end. Keep the faith.

Chapter 5

Relationships (Judges 16:4-20)

The devil wants to entice you and find where you're weak because if he finds that, then he thinks that he has you or will try to overpower you in your weakness. Delilah asked Samson time and time again where his strength lay until he gave in. Delilah wanted to know where his strength lay and the moment she knew, she told the Philistines to come to get him. They brought her the money they promised her. Samson should have seen that she was up to no good by how she tried to get him each time he told her a lie. Don't give in when the enemy tries to get you to do something out of God's will. The enemy will try to use the word love to get you to do the opposite of what you know is right or try to make you feel guilty. He will press on you so much until you do what he wants you to do. Stand strong in your faith! Samson was blinded by love and shared information with Delilah that he shouldn't have and that led to his downfall. He loved her and gave his heart to her, but sometimes we can give our heart to the wrong person. We get tied up in the wrong relationships whether that be a friendship, a business relationship, or romance. Know when to share and who to share information with because everybody is not for you. They just want to see what they can get from you.

Some people just want to see your weakness. The devil will try to plot on your weakness or where you are vulnerable, but when you are weak God is strong. If you're struggling in a certain area, you need the right people praying for you and that is not going to talk about you behind your back or use it against you. We have to be connected to the right people. Some people are just for a season. Not everyone will go where God is taking you. Know when to walk away. Some people only want to take from you and will not help build you up.

You can't share your dreams and goals with everyone because not everyone sees those dreams you have in you. So they will say negative things to you to try to keep you from doing it, to try to keep you down, and keep it from happening, and speak things on you. Look what happened to Joseph when he told his brothers his dreams. But God's plan still happened in the end. Sometimes we can let our own thoughts get in the way. Some people want to destroy your peace, some just want money, some want to pull you away from God, some just don't like you for no reason at all.

There are also times when people do things and they don't know what they are doing. That's why we have to be alert in the Spirit and know how to go about handling certain situations. Sometimes the devil is just trying to throw you off course. Some things we just have to pray about and ask God to give us the wisdom on how to handle it. Maybe some people on your job are getting on your nerves, it could be a neighbor, maybe somebody said something and doesn't know what they said, maybe it's how they said it. But sometimes God wants you to get rid of the things that are having a negative effect on you. God doesn't want us to bring old things or carry anything negative into our future so we should want the same for ourselves. The Bible says to lay aside every weight and sin which would so easily beset us and run the race with patience that is set before us. (Heb. 12:1)

After they cut his hair, Samson thought he still had his strength and there he was heartbroken and at his lowest point. Sometimes we get in relationships and get our hearts broken by letting the wrong person in. But God! He is the one who can mend your heart back together again. Do yourself a favor and save yourself from heartache and stress that comes with the wrong relationships and doing the wrong things. You know sometimes that you are getting involved with the wrong people and sometimes you are doing the wrong things. You know he was only using you and vice versa, you know that it wasn't a good business deal, you knew if you started hanging around that person they were going to try to get you to do the wrong things. You knew that man was married and vice versa... stop wasting your time!

Chapter 6

Give Birth To It (Luke 1:6-64)

Elizabeth was barren and infertile and both she and her husband were in their old age. Zacharias saw an angel and because this was something he had never seen before and something he never experienced, he became fearful. Many of us are experiencing something new now and something we have never seen before with Covid-19, but the Lord says fear not.

Even though Zacharias and Elizabeth were in their old age and she was barren, God said he had heard his prayer and that Elizabeth will conceive. Even though it seems like nothing is happening and hope is lost, God has heard your prayer and he will answer and you shall have joy and gladness. God is shifting things in our favor. Gabriel had to close Zacharias's mouth because he didn't believe it. Be careful of what you speak this season because you can mess it up, the power of life and death is in the tongue.

Both were walking upright before God, yet they had no child. Many of us feel like we're doing all that is right, but feel like something is not coming together or we're at a standstill. There is about to be a breakthrough. Elizabeth had a breakthrough after all those years of being barren, she gave birth. Likewise, the baby is about to leap out of us, we are about to give birth to some new ideas, new ways of doing things, new business, new talent & creativity.

God is doing a new thing; we have to take that leap of faith. God is birthing something in us. We are about to give life to something. Break through generational curses. We are going through the brick wall. Leap for joy! Because God is doing it. We may not see it yet, but we walk by faith and not by sight. When it became time for Elizabeth to give birth she brought forth a son. Some people will rejoice with you when you give birth to what God has for you, but not everyone. On the eighth day, they came to circumcise the child to put off the flesh. Some of us need to put off the flesh and let God cleanse us. But they tried to call him by his father's name. Some people will call you this and that and write you off. Elizabeth said, "No, his name will be called John." But no one in the family was called John. So the people wondered why John because no one in the family was called by that name. God is getting ready to use you to break the barriers in your family and new things are getting ready to happen. Zacharias confirmed the name and his tongue was loose.

Chapter 7

Prophesy To It (Ezekiel 37:1-10)

God is doing a new thing in this season and hour. He says remember ye not the former things nor consider the things of the old. Behold, I do a new thing. Now it shall spring forth. Shall ye not know it? I will even make a way in the wilderness, and rivers in the desert. (Is. 43:18-19) He sent rivers to the desert because water represents life and the Spirit of God. You may be going through a dry place in your life where it seems like hope is lost. Ezekiel was taken to the valley of dry bones where death was all around and it seemed like hope was lost. God asked him, "Can these dry bones live?" Then, he told him to prophesy to it and when he did they came together. There was a rumble and a shaking. God is shaking up some things in your life right now where you feel like things are falling apart, but it's falling into place. God's plan is still at hand. Then, God blew His breath in them and they stood up. God is raising up an army in this season. The power of life and death is in the tongue. Speak life over your situation, life over your finances, life your job, life over your business. Whatever your valley may be, speak life over it. Use your weapon! For the weapons of our warfare are not carnal, but mighty through God to the pulling down of strongholds. (2 Cor. 10:4) Pray without ceasing and watch God do it. (1 Thes. 5:17)

Chapter 8

Faith (Heb. 11:1)

Now faith is the substance of things hoped for and the evidence of things not seen. For by it, the elders have obtained a good report. What are you believing in God for? It's going to be your faith that is going to carry you through. Now faith! We are going to need it right now. Faith to see things that are unseen. For the things that we see are temporal and the things that are unseen eternal. (2 Cor. 4:18) We are going to have to move with faith this season. The ark wasn't built in a day, but Noah knew what God had told him. The people talked about him and laughed at him. Go ahead and let them talk about you and laugh at you, but make sure you're hearing the voice of God and following His instructions. For the word of God says obedience is better than sacrifice. (1 Sam. 15:22)

Nehemiah didn't come down from the wall even though the enemy tried to distract him. Don't be distracted this season. Don't let the enemy trick you into thinking it's not going to happen. Don't let the enemy hinder or conceal what God has put in your heart and what he has told you. The devil only wants to hinder what's inside of you. He comes to steal, kill, and destroy. (John 10:10) But they had a mind to work and continued to pray. (Neh. 4:6) We have to continue to pray because God answers prayers. If you want to see a change, pray and believe. Therefore, I say unto you whatsoever things you desire when you pray, believe that you will receive them and you shall have them. (Mark 11:24) On the day of Pentecost, they were all on one accord in one place speaking in tongues as the Spirit of God gave them utterance. The Bible says, "Build up yourself up on your most holy faith praying in the Holy Spirit." (Jude 1:20) The people came from abroad wondering what was this noise. It was a sound of faith going on. Will your faith make noise?! Will your faith compel the people to come? For we walk by faith and not by sight. (2 Cor. 5:7)

It was a sound to confirm that God said I will pour my Spirit on all flesh and your sons and daughters shall prophesy! For without faith it is impossible to please Him. (Heb. 11:6) If you want to please God show Him your faith. For if you have faith as a grain of a mustard seed you shall say unto this mountain remove and it shall be removed. (Matt. 17:20) For the just shall live by faith. (Rm 1:17)

He said if we have faith as a mustard seed because a mustard seed is the smallest seed, but when sown in good ground and is grown, it is the greatest. (Matt. 13:31-32) If we sow in faith on good ground we shall reap a great harvest. Don't let your seed fall by the wayside and neither let the devil snatch what was placed in your heart. When trials and tribulations come don't be offended, but stand on the word of God. Activate the holy ghost power on the inside of you. God has given us the power over all the power of the enemy to tread on scorpions and serpents and nothing by any means shall hurt or harm you. (Luke 10:19)

We have faith to move mountains if you believe you shall receive. God has given us everything we need. We have this hidden treasure on the inside of us. When God created us, he took some of Him and made us. We have greatness on the inside of us. For we are made in His image and likeness. (Gen. 1:27) God will take the bad things away. The doubt, the fear, and unbelief, and He will make you new. Stand on His word. Be ye steadfast, unmoveable, always abounding in the work of the Lord knowing that your labor is not in vain. (1 Cor. 15:58) Take Him at His word and believe and walk in it. Don't be moved by what you see or hear. Know the voice of the Lord. For my sheep know my voice and they shall not heed unto another. (John 10:27) God has given us an inheritance, live in it! He came that we might have life and have it more abundantly. Rest in the finished work and greater works we shall do because he goes unto the father. (John 14:12) Eyes haven't seen and ears haven't heard. Seek the Lord and His righteousness daily and be led by the Spirit. Fix your eyes on Him and look neither to the left nor the right. Be not concerned with the affairs of this world. Build your hope on eternal things. Run after God. Even now he is doing it according to your faith. Arise in faith and you shall see what looked impossible be possible. Victory is yours.

Chapter 9

Testimony

It took faith to write this book. Throughout the years, I would read the Bible and keep a journal of what God was speaking to me and saying. The small paragraphs begin to get longer and I thought to myself, I should write a book. I never acted on it, it was just a thought. I would read and then put my pen to paper every time God spoke to me through the years which is how this book came to be. One day, I had a dream this year in October, this lady whom I do not know and had never seen before, told me firmly, "You better start that book before the end of this year is out." I woke up and said, "Ok Lord, you must really want me to write this book." So as we do, here I go wondering about how to do it and how it will all come together. Thinking about the size of the book and so on…all the things that don't matter. What really matters is that we are obedient to God.

It took faith to move from Port Arthur, TX to Georgia. Georgia wasn't my first pick, I had California on my mind, but when I came to Georgia this particular time I didn't have anything to lose. I was laid off from a full-time job in Port Arthur and shortly after Hurricane Harvey hit Texas which affected the area I was staying in at the time. So I began to apply for jobs. I started working jobs with contracts that would last for three and sometimes six months, but never got hired full-time anywhere. I was hired for a seasonal position around Christmas, but they were so impressed with my work that they asked me to stay part-time after Christmas. From there, I worked full-time contract positions during the day and at night and on the weekends, I would work my part-time job. I held onto this job in case the others didn't work out like before. At least, I knew I would still have this job and some income. You can't always leave just because you don't like your situation. When things got rough, when I couldn't get a full-time job and chaos and confusion were all around, I kept pushing.

I overheard a conversation on the job one day where the manager was talking to one of the employees saying, "Go back to Texas" and laughing. I knew they were talking about me and I believe it was that same day or a few days later that, as soon as I left, I received a phone call saying that that was my last day. Unbothered, I said, "Praise the Lord, what's next?" Because sometimes the people you work with on the job can make it unpleasant to be there and when others wanted me to go back home to Texas, I kept the faith and accepted the challenge. Some of us need to show the devil who we are. Show the devil you are not weak! Show the devil you are not giving up. Show the devil he is a liar!

As time went on, I saw this position online for a company that I thought would be a great company to work for in my field of education. I went to the interview, but didn't receive the position. I saw the same position with the same company again for another location that was closer to where I was staying. I went to the interview, but still didn't receive the position. When I saw that I had x amount of dollars, I said now it's time to go back to Texas. The Monday before I went back, I decided to look online for jobs one more time. I came across the same position and same company again at another location about twenty minutes away from where I was staying. At this point, I'm thinking to myself, "I've already applied with this company, and for this position twice... What's the point in applying? I sat on the bed looking at my computer screen for a while and decided to go for it, "Why not, it's not that far! I'm on the way back to Texas on Monday, if nothing happens, then fine." I put in my application and had an interview Friday before the Monday I drove back to Texas. Look how God worked it out! He let me have the interview right before I went back to Texas and God blessed me to have the same part-time job with the same company that I left Georgia with.

Then, I began to think, alright Lord, what's going on? I thought to myself I guess this is it for a while. But God showed up right on time. I had a dream and in this dream, my daddy had accepted this new position that was out of the state of Texas and we were sad that he was leaving and were saying our goodbyes. I knew God was talking about me because my daddy was retired and he wasn't leaving the state. I sent the man who interviewed me a thank you email and he responded back and he told me that I was still being considered for the position. Can I tell you it's not over yet! God still has his hand on you.

It's not over until God says it's over! Don't give in just yet! God is still watching over his word to perform it. (Jeremiah 1:12) About a month later after returning to Texas they called me for the job! I'm talking about being set up by God for something greater. Yes, I've applied for jobs in Texas. I've applied in Houston, Austin, and Dallas. I've even applied for a few jobs in California and New York, but God didn't open the door there. He opened it where he wanted me to be. As a matter of fact, I've never received a phone call or an email back from those companies that I've applied for in Texas, California, and New York. So while they were talking about me behind my back and wanting me to go back to Texas for good, they couldn't keep me from Georgia. They may have let me go from a job in Georgia, but they couldn't keep me from Georgia. They may have tried everything they could to get me to go back, but they couldn't.

I have a word for you. You're going to be where God wants you to be whether the devil likes it or not. God has the final say! Keep the faith! When the devil wants you to go back to those old wasteful places and how you used to be, tell him you are not giving up just yet! When the devil wants you to pick up that bottle again, or those bad habits, or go back to that drug addiction, show him you're still in the fight! When he wants to play with your mind, thoughts, and emotions tell him you're not going there today. Stay in the race. The race is not given to the swift nor to the strong, but to those who endure to the end. (Ecclesiastes 9:11) Endure for a little while, for this light affliction shall not be compared to the worthy glory of God. (2 Cor. 4:17) You are the head and not the tail, above only and not beneath. (Deuteronomy 28:13) Darkness is under your feet.

Tell the devil you are not going back to that, tell him you're not going back to the old way of thinking, that's under your feet! Negative thoughts are under your feet. Positive thoughts are yours! Depression is under your feet. Joy is yours! Sickness is under your feet. Good health is yours! Poverty is under your feet. Wealth is yours! Fear is under your feet. Confidence is yours! You're not going back to drugs. Sobriety is yours! Doubt is under your feet. Assurance is yours! Tell Satan, get thee behind me!

If I had given up too early and gone back home, I probably would have missed the opportunity. Don't be so quick to run when things don't go right. Going back is easy, show the devil you are going to fight. The devil thought he had you and he thought he won, but the devil is a liar. Working for this company wasn't the only reason why God opened the opportunity for me here because this company is everywhere. I've applied twice and didn't get the job, but I believe God wanted to connect me with the right people. Just like Abraham when God told him to leave his country and family and go into a new land. (Gen. 12:1) God is getting ready to do new things for you and bless you. He is getting ready to elevate you. He is going to use you to do new things on Earth, new things at your job, new things in your business, and new things in your family, and what was once familiar won't be the same.

It took faith to start my small business selling handmade bath and body products. I didn't have this in mind, but I was getting ready to graduate college with my first degree and a guy asked me what I was going to do. I said, "I'll probably get a job as an administrative assistant somewhere." He said, "Think big." I thought to myself he was right. I came home thinking of all the products I could create. I did one product that I no longer carry, but as I began to mix and put things together and be more creative, I found out that I really enjoyed it. From that product, I started making more and who would have thought I would have as many amazing products as I have now. I didn't, and back then I wasn't thinking about making it. I looked at my products once and had to stop and tell God thank you. The business is probably not where you want it to be, but you have it. You made it this far. The job is probably not what you want, but thank God you have one. The car is probably not the one you want, but thank God you have something to get from point a to point b.

Yeah, I've been let down and had to hear some of the unpleasant comments people make about nobody wanting that. But the devil will have people make comments to try to distract you. They pretend they want to support you and ask for what you have under five dollars to go on and say you're not making money from that because it's only five dollars. That's because some people don't want to see you prosper plain and simple. Do what you love to do and don't worry about the rest because your gift shall make room for you and bring you before great men. (Proverb 18:16) God didn't give you that creativity for nothing, God didn't give you that talent for nothing, and God didn't give you those skills for nothing. God didn't put that desire in your heart for nothing and he didn't give you that knowledge for nothing. It's not where I want it to be, but I'll keep doing it because I enjoy it and make some decent money on the side. It's a good feeling when people who had my products before calling me from Houston, TX years later inquiring about my products. These people say that they have been trying to contact me and they're glad my number is still the same. Or when someone asks you if you're still doing your business because they wanted to get a specific product. Or when someone says you should do this product all year round. To know that the products I have made are blessing someone is a great feeling. So don't let the enemy discourage you. You don't know how your products or services will help someone and not only that, but you may inspire others. Get your passion back! You're going to have to step out on faith and do something you have never done before. Who said it was just about you? God has people connected to you and when you get onboard, they all come onboard. They all come from afar. They come from the North, South, East, and West. Arise and shine, for your light has come and God's glory shall be seen upon you. Look around and see all that comes (Is. 60:1-5). Get ready for abundance! Get ready for the overflow! Get ready, get ready, get ready. Your time is coming. Just like Simon and his partners, when they let their nets down at God's word, they enclosed a multitude of fishes. (Luke 5:4-7) You're getting ready to be blessed beyond measure.

Made in the USA
Columbia, SC
08 June 2025

59005403R10017